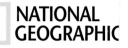

NATIONAL
GEOGRAPHIC

Plants in the Park

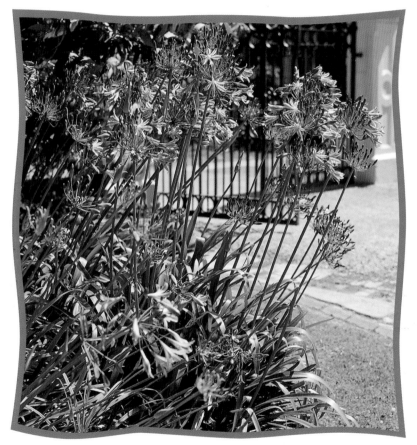

Dimi Stanos

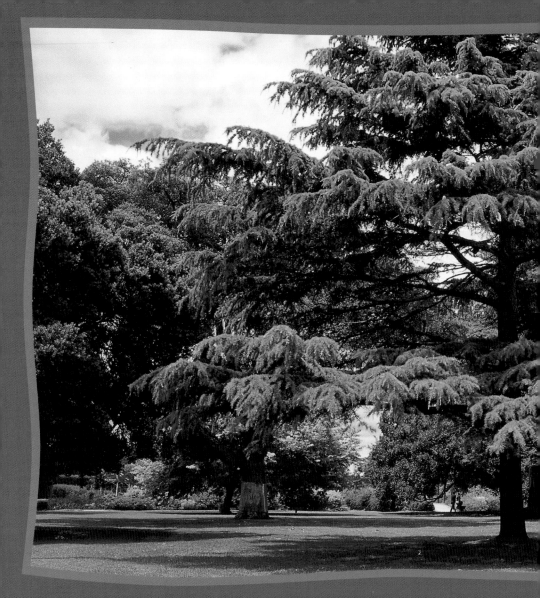

Plants grow in the park.

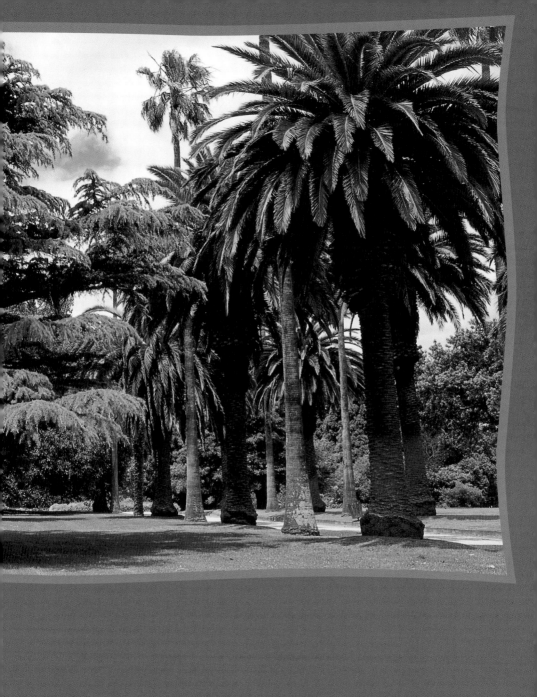

3

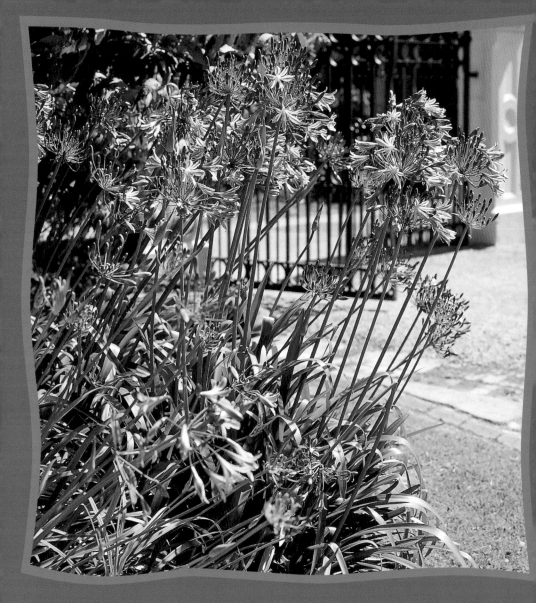

This plant grows in the park.

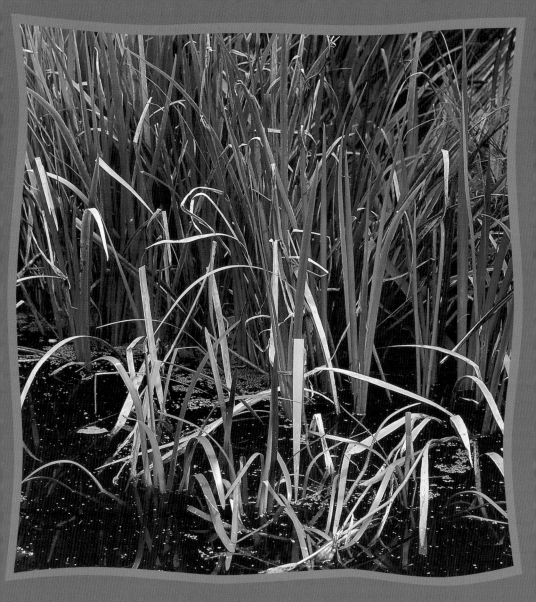

This plant grows in the park.

This plant grows in the park.

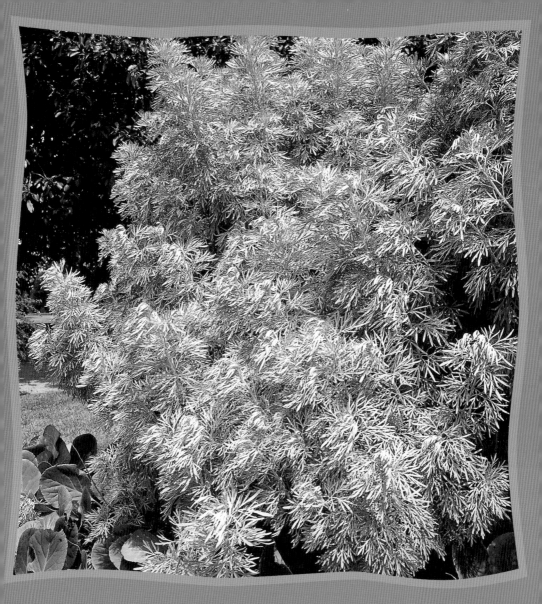

This plant grows in the park.

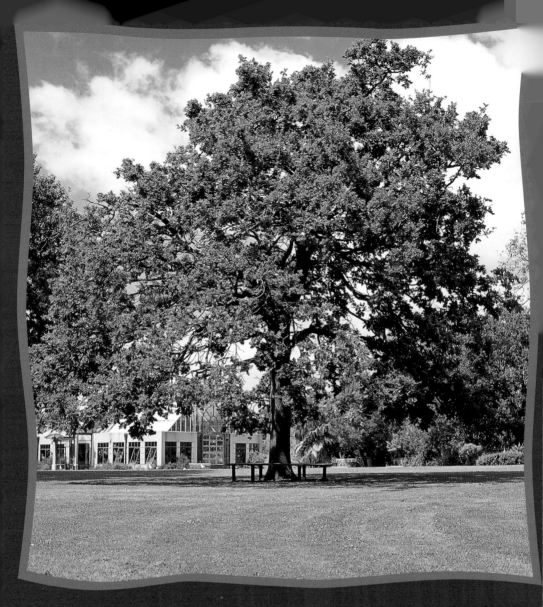

This plant grows in the park.